The Cosmic Playbook:

30 Mini Meditations for Love, Hope and Courage

P.K. Davies

Reader reviews:

"Love this little gem of a book full of helpful, daily affirmations... a great way to start your day and end the evening on a positive note."

"This delightful book is written in a simple, elegant style that makes changing your thoughts easy. The mini meditations are truly that, quick. I easily incorporated new ones into my daily routine. As an intuitive teacher and hypnotist affirmations and meditation are extremely important for me to share with my clients. Priya's Cosmic Playbook is going to be a book that I recommend often."

Keridak Silk

"I really like the 'mini' aspect of these meditations as they encourage me to practice more. These meditations are like a snack that you enjoy during many parts of the day. Very digestible and delightful."

Ramesh Dontha, Author of the #1 Best Seller: The 60 Minute Startup; Host of 'The Agile Entrepreneur' podcast

JOYFUL LIFE MASTERY BOOKS

Copyright © 2019 by P.K. Davies

www.JoyfulLifeMastery.com

ISBN 9781777052515

All rights reserved. No part of this publication may be reproduced, distributed, or transmitted in any form or by any means, including photocopying, recording, or other electronic or mechanical methods, without the prior written permission of Joyful Life Mastery, except by a reviewer, who may quote brief passages in a review.

Book Website and Newsletter:

www.joyfullifemastery.com

For my children...

"I have lived with several Zen masters – all of them cats."

Eckhart Tolle

Ignite: The Path to a Magical Life

Quest 1

Manifesting should be fun!
We know that life, change and transformation can carry their own type of growing pains.
All the more reason to find more ways to make the process of transformation enjoyable.

Jump into an adventure like no other…

IGNITE: The Path to a Magical Life

Go on fun manifesting Quests, each of which will change your life.
PLUS collect surprise manifesting gifts, trophies and badges after each Quest.

In the next few months, your friends and family will be amazed at the changes in your life.

But more importantly, you'll be living with a sense of adventure and clarity – and creating your magical life, step-by-step.

Quest 1 has been gifted to you – The Cosmic Playbook, which adds a burst of gentle positivity into your journey.
Each Quest will start with the following image. And at the end of each Quest, you will have a lovely gift to collect.

I wish you so many inspired adventures in your journey!

With much love,
PK Davies

Quest 1
THE COSMIC PLAYBOOK

Journey to Joy...

Daily inspiration to power your journey. Mini meditations, affirmations and intentions that spark loving mindfulness and self-awareness each day.

At the end of The Cosmic Playbook, you will find your secret link and magic password. Use them to collect your surprise gift and your Quest 1 trophy.

Ignite
THE PATH TO A
MAGICAL LIFE

Table of Contents

Introduction 1

1 - Mind 6

2 - Creative Energy 8

3 - Clarity 10

4 - Refocus 12

5 - Focus 14

6 - Wisdom 16

7 - Thinker 18

8 - Good Things 20

9 - In Charge 22

10 - Receiving Compliments 24

11 - Giving Compliments 26

12 - Deserving Compliments 28

13 - Worthy of Compliments 30

14 - Enjoy Compliments 32

15 - Appreciation 34

16 - Self care 36

17 - Tuning into Self care 38

18 - Nourish 40

19 - Intellect 42

20 - Spirit 44

21 - Senses 46

22 - Balance 48

23 - Caring & Love 50

24 - Completion 52

25 - A New Day 54

26 - Creativity 56

27 - Talent 58

28 - Onwards 60

29 - Kindness 62

30 - My Body 64

Intentions 66

Clearing And Energizing Abundance Affirmations 69

Thank You 75

About P.K. Davies 76

Other Manifesting Tools by PK Davies 77

The Law of Attraction Game Book 1 80

Introduction

Welcome to the Cosmic Playbook!

L ife carries many challenges, we are in a co-creative Universe after all. Even our own personal growth can be painful at times as we move through one level to another.

From childhood onwards, certain experiences can lock us into a state of anxiety or box us into a very specific way of seeing ourselves. Most of us have issues with ourselves – a critical viewpoint of our looks, abilities and opportunities. Even though this is all too human, it can hold us back from living our lives in a way that is joyful and meaningful.

Moving out of a dissatisfied stage and into love and appreciation takes more than a single affirmation – although affirmations in themselves are powerful indeed.

Does the path lie in moving through each stage of Life, powered by transformation? I think it does.

We can move through negative perceptions of ourselves to acceptance, from acceptance to like, and from like to love. Moving, opening, and flowering.

Expansion of our inner selves happens when we engage with Life and grow along the way, even though it can sometimes be painful.

The path to self-love resembles the path to a deep love relationship. It can be tumultuous but rich, profound and deeply rewarding. The only difference, of course, is that we can release a relationship with someone else, but never with ourselves. All the more reason to accept every aching, tender and poignant part of ourselves.

With the onslaught of multiple media and consumer messages showering us with comparisons that don't make us feel very good, it's imperative that we're ever more present within our lives to ensure that we aren't in a constant state of dissatisfaction.

The path to love isn't a one-off cure that can solve all our problems in one swoop – but a daily practice. It's a practice that helps to drown out all the societal noise out there - a practice that keeps us grounded yet elevated, so we can finally jump into the life adventures we wish to take.

This little love book was created as a companion to The Law of Attraction Game Book Series: Feel Great About Yourself, 2 fun handbooks with daily tasks to boost and manifest love and appreciation. At the end of this book, I've added several chapters from The Law of Attraction Game Book as a sample for your enjoyment!

In this particular book, Vital Affirmations from the Game Book are enhanced into a unique blend of mini meditations, expanded affirmations and intentional reflections.

Each mini meditation can be read once a day, or you can have fun picking them out randomly. Set an intention to invite in the meditation that will be most helpful for you that day. You can probably gobble up this book in 30 minutes. I suggest to carefully read the intention and then simply spend 2-3 minutes reflecting on it and basking in its energy.

Treat yourself to a 5-minute ritual. Centre yourself by breathing deeply three times and release any physical or mental tension. Shake your limbs slightly. If you had a busy time before you settle down to read, enjoy a moment of stillness and silence first to just BE.

Once your body feels more relaxed, look around you and feel into an awareness of your present moment. Notice the sounds, the smells, the colors and your surroundings.

Then read the mini meditation to yourself. Perhaps you can read one in the morning and one before bed.

Enjoy what feels best to you and don't be afraid to shake it up for variety!

Are you ready? :)
Then let's dive in!

1 - Mind

I LOVE MY POWERFUL MIND!

I breathe in deeply and release all thoughts from the present moment. My thoughts float like clouds in a cerulean blue sky.

I can see them, I can feel and even hear them, but today I let them be. I'm bigger than my thoughts.

If any of them get troublesome, I flick them away and they disappear...poof!

But if my thoughts are helpful, I enjoy their company and take action as needed.

I'm aware of my mind and my thoughts, and I take charge of redirecting them from this day forward.

2 - Creative Energy

I AM A CREATIVE BEING AND I ALLOW THE FLOW OF NEW AND WONDROUS CREATIONS THROUGH ME.

As I breathe in, I allow Universal energy to filter through me.

I invite in the courage to take steps towards value and meaning, even if it's taking a step that's out of my comfort zone.

I create and offer that which will enhance my life and that of others.

As I breathe out, I release old and stagnant ideas that no longer serve me and that have been holding me back.

I breathe in again and feel the rush of creative energy moving through my head, energizing my brain cells.

Oh, I love letting ideas percolate so I can create something new and fresh!

3 - Clarity

MY MIND IS CLEAR AND FOCUSED!

I run through the list of possibilities for today in my mind.

Things that I'm going to work on, play with, create and do.

It's so easy for me to pick just one to start.

I'll pick the main one – the big one – the step, the idea or the action that will work towards the life I'm manifesting.

And I'll shine through my daily work and serve, with the highest of intentions to provide value in everything I do.

I will concentrate on each of these with my full attention, knowing that as I do, I am also giving them my love and clarity and focus.

4 - Refocus

Every day, it gets easier to direct my mind wherever and whenever I choose.

I'm learning more every day, and I'm getting better at refocusing. I know that what is called "negativity" is simply something that I will now look at in the moment with curiosity.

And then I will make a decision on how to respond in a way that best aligns with my life and direction - and for the highest good of all.

This does not mean avoiding or ignoring what has come to pass. It does mean responding in a way that is for the highest good.

Each day, I commit to release stored struggle and pain that are part of my past from my cells. They find safe transport through and out of my body.

And as they leave me, I feel lighter and at ease.

5 - Focus

It gets easier to think about what I want!

As I breathe in, I allow myself to think about how I'd like to BE today and what I'd like to do.

As I breathe out, I release any past tendencies to worry about an undesirable outcome or future. I know that worry is fear based, after all, and who really knows what the future will bring?

Why clutter it up with fears? And why not think about what would be better?

More fun? More rewarding?

Breathe in...calm, ease.

I am aligning myself right now and I'm going to master the day!

6 - Wisdom

I AM A GENIUS AND I APPLY MY WISDOM*

I cradle so much potential within this earth-body.

I hold the power to envision and create. I embody natural wisdom gained from years of experiences, perhaps even lifetimes.

And I also hold a brilliant potential that is ignited

by my attention to it, and fired by focused action.

I find ways to nurture my intelligence.

I find books and exercises to spark my mind.

I carefully select what I believe, and I find new and creative ways to apply what I learn.

*This amazing affirmation is from Dr DeMartini

7 - Thinker

I AM A SMART AND POWERFUL THINKER

It's easy for me to direct my mind to the right kind of fuel for it. I'm able to cut right through into the heart of the matter and view something – anything - from various angles and viewpoints.

Regardless of my past, I recognize that I'm actually pretty smart.

I know a lot more than I realize.

And I'm even smarter by way of understanding how much *more* there is to learn.

This knowledge alone humbles me.
I love directing my mind and guiding it towards powerful brain food!

8 - Good Things

I AM FOCUSED ON THE GOOD THINGS IN LIFE!

I breathe in. This beautiful Universe is filled with everything my mind can imagine and more!

But I know that there are things that are out of my control.

I consciously decide to take action on what I can truly help with, in a way that benefits us all.

And as I breathe out, I release all that I cannot control or change.

As I breathe in, I gently move my focus to all the good things in my life.

There are so many people that I love! There is so much in my life that I value!

There is so much that I appreciate!

9 - In Charge

I am in charge of my mind

Breathe in...I focus on what's important around me.

Breathe out...I release what I cannot change.

Breathe in...I decide what I'll focus on right now.

Breathe out...I release old mental patterns that don't help me.

Breathe in...I'll control the direction my mind takes.

Breathe out...Not that way! This way. ☺

Back to what I desire to create, to do, to offer, to experience.

Back to what feels good and right and is actionable!

10 - Receiving Compliments

I LOVE RECEIVING SINCERE COMPLIMENTS!

Today I reflect on all the compliments I've received lately. Something lovely that I've been told about myself, my personality or something I did.

In fact, I'll pick one of them right now.

I pluck one like a precious jewel from the ether of my memory field. I hold it between my fingers and gaze at it from all angles.

It is a precious gift indeed.

Crafted from kindness and fired with authentic connection to a sparkling and loving brilliance!

11 - Giving Compliments

I LOVE GIVING A SINCERE COMPLIMENT TO OTHERS!

It's easy to recognize something lovely in my family members. I'm thinking of one of them now...I'm smiling...thinking of their adorable quirks.

I can see something admirable now in almost everyone I meet.

And each day, it gets easier and easier to share it with someone.

I only ever share a compliment that is genuine...something from my heart, my soul.

It gifts the lightest of all touches - a glimmer of love and connection.

12 - Deserving Compliments

I DESERVE ALL THE COMPLIMENTS I RECEIVE!

I breathe in a compliment I received recently. I breathe it in deeply, straight through my outer psyche and deep into the depths of my inner universe.

I feel a surge of love and connection from my navel and it makes me smile.

I breathe out any barriers to acceptance, anything from my past that hindered compliments from dancing their way into my heart.

I breathe in the energy of deservingness.
I breathe out any fears.

Breathe in. Breathe out.

13 - Worthy of Compliments

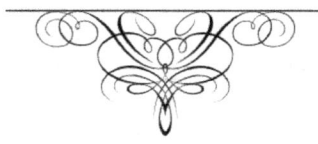

I AM WORTHY OF EVERY SINGLE COMPLIMENT I RECEIVE!

Yes.

This is the fear that I release, now and forever.

The unworthiness, the bashfulness, the shyness, the doubt, the "thanks BUT…" when I receive a compliment.

I breathe it out, all of it.

I AM WORTHY

I breathe this truth in, deeply. I let it settle down, down, into my bones.

Into my cells.

Into the magnificence of who I truly am.

Of whom we all are.

14 - Enjoy Compliments

I LOVE HOW EASY IT IS TO ENJOY A SWEET COMPLIMENT!

Aaah, it's so much easier to receive compliments now!

I have given the compliments I receive a magical power surge.

They dash through and into me. They dart around any lingering doubts, and they multiply into starburst deep within me.

The starburst blossoms into waves, small at first, then many more.

The wave of delight swells and crests into my smile and surges through my eyes.

I accept and enjoy this sweetness!

15 - Appreciation

I LOVE SHARING APPRECIATION!

It's all in the attention. The noticing. And I'm taking the time to observe.

I pull my appreciative thoughts out from within into an invisible energy swirl, a gentle misty manifestation I can fashion into whatever shape I desire.

I gaze at this little mist in my mind's eye and pat it into place with my fingers, play with it, gift it.

What a simple exchange – observed through the outer, translated and played with through the inner world, and manifested back – yet it's all composed of the stuff of love.

16 - Self Care

I LOVE TAKING CARE OF MYSELF!

I am a world unto itself within a larger, expansive Universe. When I take care of myself, it affects the greater world around me.

From within to without.

Today, it will be fun and easy to think of ways to take good care of myself. And I do it because it feels wonderful.

Today, I re-commit to being a wonderful caregiver to myself.

I forgive myself for the past.

I pledge to be responsible with myself, loving with myself and thoughtful about everything I do for myself.

17 - Tuning into Self care

I TUNE INTO MY BODY, MIND AND SPIRIT STATES WITH EASE.

I breathe deeply and begin a journey in my mind's eye...

I travel within and sense each of my organs, sending them love as I continue. I draw my attention upwards and into my mind state.

What have I been thinking about?

What would I enjoy thinking about?

Then that's what I'll do!

I continue to travel out through my senses, and I take stock of the energy field surrounding me.

How do I feel today? How would I like to feel?

So be it, so it is.

18 - Nourish

I CARE ABOUT WHAT I EAT AND DRINK.

I FEED MY BODY WITH LOVE.

I am creating a beautiful balance between nourishment and enjoyment. Sometimes, they are one and the same!

I love sinking my teeth into fresh, ripe fruit.

Or sipping a power-packed smoothie loaded with ripe berries and other healing fruit.

I can feel my cells regenerating as this nectar travels down my throat and into my body.

I welcome in the energizing vibrance of vegetables, and the soothing rainbow of other foods and beverages that I enjoy and suit me well.

I love drinking lots of fresh, pure water. My cells love it too!

19 - Intellect

I DIRECT WHAT I FOCUS ON.

I FEED MY INTELLECT WITH KNOWLEDGE AND INTERESTING TOPICS!

As the manager of my mind and intellect, I am drawn to creative content that either fuels my intelligence or relaxes me with entertainment. I get to choose.

It's easy for me to release what does not benefit me or add value to my life.

I love learning new and interesting things. I love to dive deep into topics of interest, question them, research them, and see them from all angles.

The more I learn, the greater the ability I have to absorb more.

20 - Spirit

I AM ATTUNED TO MY SPIRIT AND
I TREAT IT WITH KINDNESS AND LOVE.

What a whirlwind this world can be!

How exciting life can be!

Yet in the midst of the motion, the movement,

the bustle of activity, I find my center.

I fall into myself, and out again, cradling my earth-body within my energetic arms.

Emitting love and warmth. Energy that is soothing and comforting to my spirit. And it refreshes me for another day!

21 - Senses

I FEED MY SENSES AND EMOTIONS

WITH HEALING AND DELIGHT.

Every day brings a fresh new opportunity to revel in the magic of the Universe.

The healing light of the sun, the nourishing shade of the trees.

Plants and flowers create a healing effect all their own upon my vision.

I breathe in sensory delights. I look for them and enjoy everything that pleases my senses.

The touch of something soft, the taste of something refreshing and delicious, the sounds of laughter.

The first moment of the day when I see those I love.

The fragrance of dinner wafting towards me at the end of a busy day.

22 - Balance

I AM GETTING MORE AND MORE SKILLED AT BALANCING MY LIFE.

I know what the most important pieces of my life are, and I know how to join them together to create a gorgeous life picture.

Playtime!

Rest.

Sweet rejuvenation. Deep sleep. Mindfulness.

Work.

Creating and sharing offerings of value to the world.

Time for family and friends. Music. Laughter. A little fun.

Great food and tasty beverages. Adventures and holidays.

Balance is not a static state. It is the teeter of a seesaw...

I am propelled endlessly into growth and return to refresh and soothe my soul.

23 - Caring & Love

I'm a caring and loving person.

There's always someone, somewhere who receives my care and loving attention every day.

I care about the work I do as well.

I'm loving to friends, and I care about the environment and the world.

I show my caring in different ways - with a kind word or two, with gifts, sometimes by lending an ear or sharing understanding.

And love.... oh, how I LOVE to share love now!

It's not always easy, but I'm learning how to traverse the path of love a bit better each day.

I've found the secret to love is in the loving itself and the space.

24 - Completion

It gets easier for me to finish what I set out to do!

I get better every day at minimizing distractions. Whenever I get off track, it's easy for me to get right back to whatever I was doing.

I have the best solutions at my fingertips that help me stay the course so I can continue to jump forward, increasing the power of my momentum for whatever I do.

I love the sense of satisfaction I feel when I've completed something - it's incredibly fulfilling!

25 - A New Day

I LOVE THE START OF EACH NEW DAY!

I am refreshed and renewed once again. The cares of yesterday have dimmed and are slower to return. I will release them and create a new vision for this day.

This moment carries so much power. I will set an intention for how I want to feel today.

Which steps can I take today towards my goals?

What can I focus on?

What can I really get my teeth into and enjoy?

Where can I have some fun and replenishment?

How can I infuse even more value and love into my work and services?

I'll plan them all out now and jump in!

26 - CREATIVITY

I AM CREATIVE.

I breathe in the light of Universal energy. It flows through me with gentle and loving power, switching on and electrifying my creative genius.

I was born to create!

I breathe out my ideas. Little puffs of electric awareness. They spark and grow.

I breathe in the gifts of response, of feedback, of direction. They add sparkle to my ideas. They help me tweak and chart my course on each creative offering.

I breathe out pure play and vision, now manifest in my creations!

27 - Talent

I AM A TALENTED PERSON AND I FEED MY TALENT

I bring my attention to all that I do well naturally. And from here I remember that this body of mine comes with exquisite skills.

Latent, but incredibly powerful once awakened.

Today, I will take one action to feed and nourish my talent.

I'll practice my singing, write a chapter, sketch a few lines, kick the ball around the field, shoot a few hoops, set a new dance sequence, learn something new.

And then I pledge to do the same tomorrow and the day after that.

I will take however long it takes to BE the creative force that I am!

28 - Onwards

I WALK FORWARD WITH COURAGE AND FAITH!

I breathe in Universal potential, bright with color and magic.

I let it swirl around within my energy field.

I breathe out courage.

I take the first step, then the next. Whatever clouds my view forward or hampers my progress, I will deal with in the moment.
And now, my vision is clear.

My brilliant and sparkling dreams are right here as I step into them from the sepia of the past.

And when I fall down, I know I'm not alone.
The invisible hands of loved ones help me up with infinite patience.
And my faith in my present and future pulls me forward!

29 - Kindness

KINDNESS IS A WAY OF LIFE FOR ME.

Kindness exists all around me. It's here today. I need only be still and observe kindness to understand its nature.

For within the stillness lies compassion. Deeper and vaster than I can comprehend.

A pulsing, surging, living, golden energy of infinite love.

I look for ways to express kindness in my words, my actions, my activities and with everyone I meet today.

I breathe in compassion. I breathe out kindness.

30 - My Body

I AM CREATING THE BODY OF MY DREAMS: HEALTHY, STRONG AND FIT!

Oh, I'm in this for the long game. No quick fixes.

No excuses.

No time to waste on what doesn't serve me or the world.

I do one thing every day to boost my health. I eat and drink that which nourishes me fully, even though I enjoy my treats!

I do one thing every day to strengthen my body. I walk, exercise, build, play, swim, run, dance, cycle. Whatever my body needs, I will do it.

I do one thing every day to feed myself fun and laughter.
This too is beauty, sweet and precious.

INTENTIONS

I SET MY INTENTIONS FOR EACH MOMENT.

Within this moment lies a secret. The secret to today and tomorrow.

The secret is this: The power of my intention is fueled by my attention.

And it is manifested through action.

What do I intend for this moment?

How do I choose to feel right now? How *am* I feeling?

Not that great?

If they arise from internal triggers, I will assess them in the present, deal with the situation now and make peace.

And then I'll watch a funny video or read something uplifting for a few moments.

If there's a legitimate problem I am experiencing either in my own life or in the world, I will deal with it in the most humane way possible for the greater good.

Whether that is by taking positive action.

Or with collaborative compassion for others who suffer.

What do I intend to do right now?

What would be a wonderful step forward?

Whatever that is, I take full responsibility.

I own it.

I breathe in glorious potential.

I breathe out powerful transformation.

I breathe, in rhythm with Life itself!

Clearing And Energizing Abundance Affirmations

I walk with increasing confidence into the vibrant future that I am creating,

I now clear and energize my spaces within and without.

I clear and energize my financial past, present and future.

I clear and energize my thoughts and my emotions around money.

I allow my body to return to a state of natural flow.

As within, so without.

I clear any unwanted financial memories from my past.

I cut the strings that tie these memories to my etheric state.

I allow all emotions to BE.

I allow any emotions that hold me back to gently float away.

I forgive myself now for any lingering regrets around my life.

I forgive myself now for any lingering regrets around money.

For anything I feel I should have done. Or for things I feel I should not have done.

I release the energy around hoarding and overspending.

I let it all go.

And I return to the flow of life, the flow of energy.

I release all that does not serve me. So be it, so it is.

I clear and release fears and worries around my current financial situation.

I release old money stories.

They don't matter anymore.

Today is a new day – and I am starting afresh.

From this moment onwards, I open myself to abundance.

To all the beautiful possibilities that exist.

I open myself to refreshing and interesting money-making ideas.

Some of these ideas may come through channels that already exist.

Some of these ideas will spring from my state of flow.

I intend to act upon those that offer the most value to the world, and that inspire me.

And I allow myself to fall into the flow

Each day, I release more and more that does not serve me.

I release them gently and swiftly.

And every day, it becomes easier and easier to turn my focus towards my desires.

Each day my desires become clearer and clearer. And they change over time, as they will.

I intend to set aside a little time every single day to reflect on all that I desire.

I commit to setting aside a little time every single day to work on all that I offer of value.

I know that as I do so, I draw in the immense powers of the Universe.

And I invite the Universe now to deliver abundance in all its forms.

I intend to continue to focus on my desires.

I intend to fully see and appreciate the incredible and beautiful person that I am.

I intend to use my wealth in ways that will benefit myself, my loved ones and the world.

So be it

So it is.

Thank You

T hank you for reading this little love book! When you share your Beautiful Self with the world, it contributes to this powerful Universal creative energy. You are part of Life.

I invite you to jump into the Ignite manifesting adventure!

May you shine your light bright and strong, beautiful soul!

With love,

P.K. Davies

ABOUT P.K. DAVIES

P.K. Davies creates award-winning Law of Attraction, manifesting and mindfulness books and tools. She is the creator of IGNITE: The Path to a Magical Life (a manifesting adventure).

They are designed for those who want to forge their own path and create a fulfilling, empowered and expansive life.

Joyful Life Mastery tools combine metaphysical magic with down-to-earth goal achievement and a saucy passion for personal growth. She narrates meditation audios for app companies, and currently creates guided relaxation, sleep, mystical, manifesting and affirmation audios as part of the Joyful Life mastery tools.

P.K. Davies is an author, voice artist and singer, with a degree in Psychology.
Born in England, she currently lives in Canada with her family.

Other Manifesting Tools by PK Davies

THE LAW OF ATTRACTION GAME BOOKS 1 & 2 - MODERN LAW OF ATTRACTION: FEEL GREAT BEING YOU SERIES

THE COSMIC PLAYBOOK FOR WRITERS: Daily Affirmations And Mindfulness For Authors

SCENT OF AN ANGEL - Poetry

BOLLYWOOD P.I. CALIFORNIA DREAMING: A Sizzling Mystery / Action & Adventure (as Priya Khajuria)

MANIFESTING TOOLS

IGNITE – The Path to a Magical Life

Quest 1
THE COSMIC PLAYBOOK

YOUR SECRET LINK...

https://bit.ly/38dkBO3

MAGIC PASSWORD...

lovelight

Ignite
THE PATH TO A
MAGICAL LIFE

Facebook:

Facebook.com/joyfullifemastery

Pinterest:

Pinterest.ca/joyfullifemastery

Amazon Author page:

amazon.com/author/pkdavies

THE LAW OF ATTRACTION GAME BOOK 1

Sample

Introduction

Welcome, beautiful Soul!

Today marks the day that you'll start seeing yourself in all your brightness and color. By the time you're done with this book, you'll have a new and rich appreciation for yourself, rooted in reality and proven too!

Frankly, you'll be astounded at what you discover about yourself during this Game.

To top it off, you'll lock in all that amazingness by creating a simple, Daily Power Ritual. I will walk you through all of this.

We know that...
Life isn't always easy.
We can feel fragile sometimes. Traumatic things happen.
We feel pain and we suffer. Our hearts break.

Sometimes this propels us forward, but emotional pain can often pull us back into a holding pattern.

But we are also RESILIENT.
We find courage and we rise.

We pull from our strengths and find more - so much more – determination, and we recreate our lives.

Have you ever experienced crippling anxiety, depression or had panic attacks?

You know the kind – the ones that keep you up at night staring at the ceiling. Then you google your symptoms (BIG mistake, never do that!) and end up with a BIGGER anxiety attack.

Just know that you're not alone! I had these for years too.

We all feel unnoticed, lonely, unloved or insecure at times. It's part of the human condition, but we can emerge from these states and we can *thrive*.

There is nothing to be ashamed of when you're feeling down. Give yourself a big virtual loving hug, same as if you would for a dear friend, and reach out for help when you need it.

When you need to feel those emotions, go ahead and feel them. It's your right and it's emotionally healthy to feel the feels.

Just do it and don't worry about having to be positive all the time.

Love and kindness are light and warmth that we all crave. These are the universal *sparks* that connect us all as human beings. They transcend things like religion, culture or upbringing.

Love and kindness bring us together, they inspire and transform us. Just one simple act of sharing love and kindness begins a healing process, both on the giving and the receiving end!

Support is SO important, but so is the way we support ourselves. There's a special kind of energy that comes from being the giver and receiver of love and kindness *to yourself.*

So, as you go through this Game, be kind to yourself every step of the way! Gently release any self-judgements that may arise as you go through each exercise.

It's normal to focus immediately on weaknesses we seem to have, or a body area we aren't too happy with. I'm no guru and I'm not going to be teaching you anything per se. Instead, we'll be in this together.

I'll share fun techniques and processes that helped me and many others too.

These exercises aren't going to *tell* you that you're lovable. They're going to SHOW you!

And boy, oh boy, are you ever going to FEEL it!
Are you ready to jump in?

If you'd like to read more about *how* these exercises help you, read on. Otherwise skip straight to the next section on *How to Play*.

The Power of Gentle Transformation

Alright...

Let's talk about this amazing journey of inner transformation! It can be rough; it can be easy; it can go any which way.

Want the easy-ish way?
I do! :)

Moving through the flow of self-discovery and self-love with awareness is really a gradual awakening. This flow can help us transform. And I don't mean transform into someone else; no...something much better!

You will transform into an expanded version of *yourself*!

It's through this gradual awakening and transforming light that we can gently accept and release shadows.

We can gently let go of old pain and heartbreak.
We can stop comparing ourselves to others.
We can finally let go of all that regret!
And allow healings to start inside.

But - transformation involves accepting the present moment first.

This is why so many ancient cultures practice mindfulness. When we choose what we want, how we're going to respond and what we're going to do – for stuff happening NOW, we bring this consciousness into the NOW and build our future into an expanded version of ourselves.

This doesn't mean accepting the present as the endgame. It doesn't mean that you should take crap from anyone and it doesn't erase your past.

Accepting the present simply means being aware that this moment is here – it is what it is.
For now.

By engaging with the potential of the present moment, you experience a new awareness. You create a fresh perspective from which to respond and from there move into your next moment.

Our choices and responses right now define our present and future experiences. *Awareness* is the key.

Meaning...
Let yourself BE. Right now.
Look around. Feel this moment of time.
Can you feel the air around you? The space?

In THIS second, you can pick and choose how and what you're going to do next...which is basically building your future. Isn't that just the best???

We just have to find a way to stop our old habits from taking over and running the show when it comes to how we respond.

Let's move towards seeing yourself as a Being with incredible energy and potential.

END OF SAMPLE

Visit this link to order a copy on Amazon or through online bookstores.

https://amzn.to/37bMmpG

www.ingramcontent.com/pod-product-compliance
Lightning Source LLC
Chambersburg PA
CBHW070939080526
44589CB00013B/1577